T0358143

Wakefield Press

On Luck Street

Tall when necessary, **Peter Bakowski** has been writing poetry for 41 years. He remains influenced by the following quote, attributed to Robert Frost—"Make your next poem different from your last."

In 2015 Éditions Bruno Doucey of Paris, published a bilingual selection of his poetry, titled *Le coeur à trois heures du matin*. Later this decade Éditions Bruno Doucey will publish a further bilingual selected, titled *La saison du courage*. In Australia in 2022 Recent Work Press published his poetry collection, titled *Our Ways on Earth*.

Charmless, and 'despondent' despite a seemingly endless run of luck, **Ken Bolton** managed— with an ineptitude *profonde*—Dark Horsey, the Experimental Art Foundation's bookshop—and the Lee Marvin readings. In Adelaide, a figure trailing rumour and scandal, and associated, for example, with the louche set surrounding Noah Banens, his recent collections include *Starting at Basheer's* (Vagabond) and 2022's *Fantastic Day* (from Puncher & Wattmann). Shearsman (UK) issued a *Selected Poems* in 2013, replacing an earlier Penguin *Selected*. The author's book on Life at Sea—*A Pirate Life*—was published by Cordite this year.

The complete interlinked *Elsewhere Variations* series—*The Elsewhere Variations*, *Nearly Lunch*, *Waldo's Game* and *Luck Street*—is now available from Wakefield Press.

On Luck Street

Peter Bakowski and Ken Bolton

**Wakefield
Press**

Wakefield Press
16 Rose Street
Mile End
South Australia 5031
www.wakefieldpress.com.au

First published 2023

Front cover photo 'Lunch time, Autigia, Sicily' by Mel London
Back cover photo 'Market area, Matsudo, Japan' photo by John Levy
Edited by Polly Grant Butler, Wakefield Press
Typeset by Jesse Pollard, Wakefield Press
Original design by Michael Deves, Wakefield Press

Printed in Australia by Pegasus Media & Logistics

ISBN 978 1 92304 204 9

A catalogue record for this
book is available from the
National Library of Australia

Wakefield Press thanks
Coriole Vineyards for
continued support

Contents

SIXPACK NINE

Acknowledgements

Some of these poems, or earlier versions of them, have appeared in the following magazines and journals, either in print or online: *Dreich* (Scotland); *Social Alternatives*; and *Takahē* (New Zealand).

SIXPACK ONE

Sofa ahead

Such wealth—to drift, doze, dream of oranges, consider the
Origin of the universe, an epigram by George Bernard Shaw.
Fly on the wall, perhaps it's your last day on Earth. Are you
Aware of that? If yes, then I accept your angry buzzing.

A breeze, felt on my resting brow. To rise and close the window may be
Hasty—I haven't finished admiring the ceiling—how the
Elongated shadow of my raised right hand lingers
Across its width. Twenty-five days since I've had a
Drink of rum or seen Dr. Bernhardt.

Matinee—Council Flat, Fitzroy

Early morning sun comes thru the high window. Out
in the kitchen the canary is really going off, in a big way—
jumping, I know, from perch to perch, perch to swing,
to sway there—& back, for a long declamation.
What is it, I often wonder—birds outside? It's
never anything. So it's internal. At the end
of a long morning—of these addresses to the nation—
the bird will suddenly turn quiet, fluff itself
into a ball & sit or stand, small, yellow, reflecting to itself.

I begin to thread this needle—a seam I'll catch
before the pants are unwearable or I put them
in the wash & forget them. Can I thread this thing before
the coffee begins to percolate? or the bird starts up again?

No, Eric's off—what started him?—the coffee I expect,
which is just now bubbling away. I put down the
thread & needle. Nearly had it, two or three times.
Turn the gas off. *There you go, Eric,*
I say—and "Coffee?" I offer him. He is silent.

No. No. "Not *I* don't. And *I* don't. Cause *all* I *want*
is *you*," I sing. Tho still he doesn't stir. I pick up my
gun & head out. Ha, ha—only kidding.

3

The Unburdening—A Trip To Waldo's

"Good morning. A coffee? There's something on your mind."

"Ernie's died, Waldo." "Ernie? I thought his name

was Eric?" "Ernie—Eric. He's gone now. The place is silent."

"He was a nice bird." "Better than a radio!" *"What?"*

"I mean, he was. Much better company—the talk on the wireless,

the songs, even the songs—Eric's were better—and at least

he meant them. Somehow."

"I used to think he was showing off." *"I* showed off

for him, too. We were a team." "I'll get you another."

"Thanks. How's things?"

"Stefan's Wallace has been sick, so I haven't seen them for

a little." "Well, they don't want you to catch anything." "No. Yes.

But after a few days I miss them, Wallace & his sister."

"What's her name again—'Priscilla'?" *"Rose."*

"Rose is a pretty name."

Dr. Bernhardt talks to a colleague

Initial sessions with Saahana at my Eltham Clinic—

the calibrated establishment of trust.

It was last Spring when she began talking about her parents,

the car accident, being the only survivor.

As a child, the numerous relocations—

chaotic or grim households, various aunts.

The last one, Aunt Anika, a saviour.

Patient. Playful. She taught Saahana to notice

palm trees, cloud formations, when the moon

sulked or appeared 'boastful',

and gave her lessons in breathing, meditation, balance.

Saahana studied architecture as a teenager, in New Delhi, learned—

light, air flow, perspective, the actual and visual

weight of marble, teak, glass.

Now, aged 65, Saahana still struggles with anxiety, poor self-regard.

She's always on guard, looking to be emotionally robbed.

I remind her that she's designed buildings in Bilbao, Geneva

and Kuala Lumpur which the public love and use daily.

Saahana shrugs, sometimes giggles, looks down—at the clinic carpet,

her toes, and the lime green of her favourite shoes.

Verna Tresset writes to her sister Wanda Hopkirk, 1 June 1949

My room is on the 6th floor.
I'm yet to count the stairs
or the cockroaches which hold meetings
on the window sill.

I could reside at a grander address
but living here amongst clerks and office cleaners
is my education.

A clamorous neighbourhood.
From dawn into the evening
stallholders and hawkers extol their produce—
cleaved slices of coconut, mango, watermelon.
Watch and shoe repairs are conducted on a sturdy box
positioned directly on the pavement.
Barefoot tea boys carrying laden trays,
dodge between cyclists, rickshaw drivers, wheezing buses,
to prospective customers fanning themselves in rug and sari shops.

I no longer wear jewellery or carry an appointment book.
My present wardrobe consists of a pair of closed shoes,
a pair of leather sandals, two cotton saris and an umbrella.

I've never felt so free.

Coogee—Incident on Arden Street

I'm just coming back from my afternoon walk—I do

two of them, each day—along the esplanade, the beach.

A guy pulls up, in a sleek black Audi, winds the window down

& calls me. "Hey, a word." And I amble over, frown

into the light. When I bend down the shade of the trees

enables me to see them: a tanned, moustached, Japanese

face, accent American. "One question," he says. "But first,

you're Frank Brookmeyer?" "I am," I say, "and who

are you?" "Royden Muranaka," he says, "tourist." "Two

less likely tourists …" "From *Honolulu,*" he says. "I have to wear

the Hawaiian shirt?"

"And your partner?" I indicate the guy across from him, passenger-side,

large, suited, mirror shades, looking out the other window

away from us. Bored, is the implication. "Trip Mizoguchi,"

says Royden. The larger man turns his head towards me.

The slightest of nods. A hire car, I can smell the new upholstery—faux,

or maybe real, leather. "Know the name

'Veronica Devereaux'?" "I know the name," I say,

emphasising the last word. "Question is," says the big guy

from the passenger side, "how do you know it?" "Friend of mine

passed it on," I say. "The friend being your new boss—José

7

Watchamacallit." "Félipe Perez," I supply the correction. "*Friend?*" he asks.

"Friend," I say. "Thing is," says sunglasses, "you're out here—a *long* while—

& Dr Devereaux's out here too." "I didn't know that." "We're yet to see

the connection. We're looking into it." "Major fraud, Frank—you, your boss, this

Devereaux."

"Your boss sent you instructions?" "No," I say. "I'm a cop. Dr Devereaux—real name

Veronika Stein—was a friend—& used to be my doctor. She said, 'take a rest'. Which

I'm doing. The police here have closed this case." "Except for this woman Stein, or

Devereaux."

"Well I didn't know she was here. Félipe passed the name on out of amusement, I would

guess."

"If it turns out you're involved, Frank, you'll be in trouble." "I'm not in any trouble," I tell

Royden.

I straighten up. "The police here got the money," I add. "It's not the money, Frank.

It's corruption: you, your boss Gonzalez, Dorothy Steinway …" "Listen, Motorgucchi—

it's Perez, I'm Brookmeyer, the doctor is Stein—or 'Devereaux' if you want to retain your

handicap.

And I'm almost retired. Perez is new in the job—but clean. I haven't seen or heard about

Veronika Stein in a long while." "Except for your old partner 'passing things on'. So the

connection,

we believe, is alive." "It isn't." "And yet you stay, Frank. You stay." "My leg is slowly

healing.

I've been given a great deal of leave: I'll stay here till the end of it."

SIXPACK TWO

Afternoon Sun in Glebe

I'm sitting in the kitchen looking at nothing in particular—
I know this place—then looking at the fruit in the bowl, under
the poster that's lived here forever—glued to the wall. Yellowing.
Some stains, some tears. PIG IRON BOB DEAD AT LAST, it says.
Slightly fly-blown & slightly yellow—from the stove—
but I like it, always—more than the Mao "Dare
to struggle, dare to swim", which I like too.

                                        And there—
the polished concrete near the door—'s where my friend
skidded doing a James Brown impression
and broke a louvre in the window.

                        •

I'm an alcoholic now—not on drugs anymore
… still sniff a bit of paint. School's out — I can hear the kids
yelling in the back alley, banging on the tin of the fences.

·

One time everyone came home this night

from a Hepnotics gig, big crowd of people—

Continental Robert was there—people kept doing that

falsetto he does. Or did. Does he still do it? Every

so often you'd hear someone warbling woo-oo-oo! that

high note, & there'd be laughter. A friend of mine,

my good friend ... but I told you that. Sitting here,

by the door, this bit of sun, the kids—it's the best.

Don't know when anyone's coming home. Soon, I guess.

In tune

An old coot lives in the flat below Pip's,

claims he's a poet.

Pip knows she should ask to read some of his poems,

feign a keenness to do so,

but really she's hooked on Netflix,

follows numerous Scandinavian crime series.

Blood seeping into snow—

Pip considers that poetry.

A decade now Pip's been with Yarra Trams.

The pay's great. Such a strong union.

Double rates on weekends, extra for split shifts.

A woman can think in that driver's cabin,

alone with those important-looking dials and gauges.

Maybe whistle a little—that Charlie Rich song,

"Behind Closed Doors."

On the Malabar Coast

Borgeld's strangled corpse,

found in a Singapore shipping container,

gave pause to those in Sydney and Macau

who liked breathing

and other pleasures.

Eleven months.

Not one encrypted message from Ricardo or Duc.

Shane no longer

sets up trip-wire alarms

below the windowsills

and at the bottom of the staircase

before sleeping.

Daru, the houseboy,

Shane is training him—

weekends they skip rope, do sit-ups,

practise Thai kickboxing.

Focus. Discipline. Repetition.
The goals—leanness and power,
to unnerve your opponent
by your stance and stare.

Shane is pleased with Daru's progress.
The kid has real fire in his belly.
He won't stay a houseboy much longer.

Dead Man

A cyclist appears, having crossed the train tracks,

causing the woman—tho it's not necessary—to pause when she

sees him. She looks, & he nods, & smiles, a figure

she has seen before, many times, regular,

morning & night—& still to be seen, frequently,

but, now, at *any* time. He must've retired, she thinks.

Wouldn't you ride somewhere else, *rather than*

the road to work? He might lack imagination. Still,

nice enough. The man smiles. *And he will*

not convert to lycra. It looks silly on a man,

in her view, and wrong on a woman, really, tho tights

she can approve. Black leggings or whatever,

that all the girls are wearing, she thinks, make them look

like Navy divers, or a kind of glamorous ninja—adroit,

efficacious, nimble, magnificently sinister. Neither

one of them speaks. The man is away. But she would be

content—*always*—to let him go. Acknowledged, but unspoken to.

To speak to a stranger one's own age (approximate)

is to be made suddenly aware, & no mistake,

that you share a language that is gone, that is to

disappear. And it is troubling. You will be—both of you—
gone with it. The imagined exchange, of words, of
commonplace & agreement. You realise how much your head echoes
with the repeated, tortured syntax & pronunciation
 of the television news readers, the new mannerisms of the young.

The energy that scorn requires. The terms—irritating, insidious—
can reverberate for whole mornings, afternoons, while you
despair of them: words you will never hear again, gone; & words
that make you howl inwardly—"watched on", "wreaked" (why not wrought?),
"bored of" (really?)—*absolutely* (never just 'Yes', never
certainly or true—or precisely, exactly, entirely) … answers
that begin—as tho rehearsed—with "So".

Entente Cordiale

No, address someone else old & there is mutual recognition—
you are both sidelined, you are "dead men walking".
Admittedly, *he* was riding a bike, & you are a woman.
And still pretty sharp. Alert, anyway. "It's come to this,"
she thinks, her mouth tightening, "this" being
undefined but indicating or gesturing at—(a 'mental' gesture, she thinks,
explaining this to *some*one)—her whole situation.

She bears him now some good will.

Her attention shifts—to a small girl coming toward her
on a very small white bike, who pauses, legs wide,
& waits for her mother to catch up.

The girl has auburn curls that escape her helmet (white &
pink), a white t-shirt—& watermelon overalls. Sneakers.
The mother wears tights. "Hullo."

Southeast of Christmas Island

It's been a good season.
The trawler's refrigerated hold is full.

Landfall by the end of the week,
be in port for 72 hours—
refuel, restock the kitchen,
hopefully pass the WA health and safety check.

Three days ashore. Enough time for some of the women
in the crew, to hook up with local stevedores,
miners and truck drivers.

After a couple of months, perhaps in the middle of the Pacific,
one or two will wake with morning sickness.

I still remember delivering Ula's baby—
the blood on my hands, the lurch of the trawler
as I cut the umbilical cord, the applause of the crew.

Ula's Perlita is 3 years old now, has become the trawler's mascot,
bears the nickname "Octopus"—she grabs at everything—
breasts, rosary beads, bucket handles.

Since deciding on an all women crew, I've never looked back.

There's solidarity and an armoury of skills

in mechanics, oceanography, acupuncture and karate.

My parents, both in their 80's,

and living in Perth,

will never understand me—

the decisions I make.

SIXPACK THREE

Mobile phone conversation on the No. 6 tram

Yesterday—Can you hear me?—a bunch of us had a picnic
in Edinburgh Gardens. Yes, yesterday.
Ralph wolfed down four of the curried egg and lettuce sandwiches,
before Carmel and I managed to grab one each.
Moira wasn't hungry. A modelling audition next week.
I wished her luck as she's been *so* supportive
since Jeremy dumped me. Yes. No, she has.
I go out of my way to avoid his crowd, stick to northside—
there's bound to be someone I know having a coffee at Sila
on a Saturday morning—often Bec and Monica—I think they're
still a couple, but come to think of it, Monica seemed less clingy
last time I saw them.

I've stopped seething about Jeremy. There is the barista at Waxflower.
Small tattoo of a swallow on his left wrist. Reddish hair. Long fringe.
His name's Ari. I'm on the tram to there now.

Wrestlemania

My right arm is about two thirds extended
& Georgesson can push up, but not as easily
as I can pull down. The crowd has grown quiet—
a small one, this is a Wednesday night. Friday night,
Saturday—if you got this same lull—it would be

broken up by catcalls & loud noises, even the ice-cream guy
would be heard—*"chocolate Hearts, cornettos"*. Tonight
he has gone home. They have their eye on us tho—
waiting for his arm to give. The ref keeps on the move, so
as to suggest some drama. Up towards the light,

more the closer you get to the incandescent
source of it, insects—moths I suppose—circle
& flit & flutter, bright against the darkness,
a cone of them, white—& terrified?—tho calmness
is what they communicate as they circle,

humming, praying? Dervishes do that—don't they?
Anyway, the angle of my arm above my head,
the bend at the elbow, reminds me, suddenly, of
being at work at the ICI factory, on that press. I laugh.
I hear the cry that used to go round amongst the men when

the foreman was needed. It was always sung
in comic fashion—Bill Lesley, Bill Lesley, where
are you? & the foreman would show up & a problem
would be solved. Maybe it was the late afternoon
light in the factory as closing time approached. Time here

pretty much, to bend Georgesson down to the canvas.

He's heard me laugh & is getting restive. He thinks it's
him of course. Should I tell him about Bill Lesley?
Ha ha. There we go. Arm comes down. We rise.
It's the end of the round. The crowd's amused cries
register low-level excitement when the ref Arthur Billingsley

is elbowed aside so Georgesson can give me a shove.
I laugh again, shrug. 'Giorgio' is not such a fool
usually. He's annoyed tonight. I'm thinking, tho, *Bill Lesley,*
Bill Lesley, where are you? (It was fifteen years ago, he
was thirty then. I was seventeen. We made tool

parts I think, or machines for *making* tools? I didn't
stay long & never cared to ask. I hardly care now.)
That was the last round. I'd lost count. I stand
& Arthur raises my arm in the air. I look again
at the moths. When the house lights come up—& now

they do—they'll drop down from that height ...
& *consider their options,* I guess? Flame worship,
or a bit of a rest. Is self-immolation the best
way out? I'll ask Georgesson if I see him.
And duck. Ha ha. (Home to mum.)

Berys

"Berys rang this afternoon." "'Bere*jik*lian'?"—
the kind of joke he likes to make. "Berys," she repeats,
"My sister." "Ah, yep. How is she?" "Fine."
"Want anything?" "No. Keen to talk I think.
She rabbited on. Her health: she's well; what's

in flower, what she's planning." "She's coming here?"
"No, not travel—what she'll plant. And what's growing round
the neighbourhood. She talked mostly about *grammar*—went on
at some length, about something that annoyed her.
Sounded quite happy really. Asked after the kids.
Emily in particular. She'd like to see her.
Could Emily come to her, she suggested. Actually,
she talked like a teenager. At one stage she said,
'Is that even a thing?' or 'I think
that's a thing'. Odd." "But pretty happy?"
"Yes. Would Emily like to go, do you think?"
"To Adelaide? Probably. She likes Berys."

Rani in her bedroom, 24 Gore Street, Fitzroy

12 pairs of shoes.
A potted geranium in need of watering.

And a phone call to Dad. Overdue.
He'll ask about Earl.
I'll burst into tears then. Dad
never liked him.

Books fall from my hands.
I don't want the blare of TV.

I'll take Elmo for a walk around the block.
Across the road, the neighbour,
Mr Ferber, in Number 23,
still gives me dirty looks.
Well, I can't see myself
throwing a party anytime soon.
Ferber can put down his binoculars,
wash his silver Merc on Sundays,
the orderly life.

I won't move out of Fitzroy
though I'll avoid Smith Street for a while,
Earl's favoured record shops.

Maybe tomorrow I'll start
on repainting the lounge-room.
Last month Desmond at Manfax Paints
showed me a bunch of colour cards.
There was this shade of yellow I liked.

Jeremy has a coffee with Ari at Sonido,
69 Gertrude Street, Fitzroy

Sometimes I do my thinking through my pants—

there was a house party in North Carlton.

Upmarket terrace house. They had a DJ. Bathtub full of coldies.

About 2 a.m. I started kissing a Colombian girl, Adella.

Well, Thea saw that.

I ended up walking home. Yep, all the way.

I've left, what is it…? Nine, yeah, nine voice messages.

No, not with Adella. With Thea. No reply. Nada. Zip.

I did spy Adella yesterday, in Gertrude Street,

getting into a silver Merc with two hefty shopping bags.

There was this guy, in his mid-fifties, behind the wheel,

no father vibe coming off him.

Three gold rings on his driving hand.

Hawaiian shirt. Stone bald.

I stood there slack-jawed,

should have taken a photo of the licence plate…

but that guy, some kind of heavy—

could break your kneecaps with a stare.

Notes towards a review, begun in a coffee shop, Brunswick

"I associate you—from a couple of years ago—"
Hillary's words, "with blocky, heavy concrete. *As used*
by a few others. Tho your work announced its independence
of the syntax that imprisoned theirs.

                                        Still,
a dead-end scenario," she wrote, "apparent, first,
fifty years back, when it must've been 'a crowded field'
—many ships, mapping *a harbour,* rather than
an imagined cul-de-sac."
                                        Hilly thought some more.
"Your drawing, now, is something different."

 (And she thinks to herself, I always like artists' drawings—
drawings *for* a work—they are so entirely 'idea'.)

"The drawing reminds, ... of Florine Stettheimer
At least, her name pops into my brain"

(Where it will not find much else—maybe an image or two,
that explain why 'Stettheimer' has come to mind)

(Because, I have thought of
Dorothea Tanning meanwhile—'A Little Night Music'.
The wavery lines, the plant forms (there are some vines depicted,
in the top right of yours)? Hilly stops there, aware
that her monologue is really part of the review. If it
is a review. Or is she addressing the artist?

"Your work will be sculpture—but clearly something
not playing out 'the end game of modernism'

No more concrete squares. No grid.
                                                    I'll be curious
to see what you're doing."

SIXPACK FOUR

Pleased to be out-foxed—Hilly, in Slowpoke, Fitzroy

"I visit the studio—&

there's your work

exactly as the drawing indicated," she writes, days later,

"but more immediate—real objects."

(And) *"What are you doing?*

No vine?"

Neighbours

Rani and Elmo sit out on the balcony,
both drowsy after last night's interrupted sleep,
the thunder, so loud and violent.

Mr. Ferber, from across the road, at number 23, waves to them.
He's mellowed. Now when they bump into each other,
in the dog park or out walking by the Yarra, there's small talk—
the weather, the responsibilities of dog ownership,
Melbourne's chances of winning the Grand Final…
Rani, to be polite, show an interest, recently asked him
"What's your field of employment?" Ferber had looked away,
down at the gold rings on his right hand, mumbled "Debt Collection".
Then, perhaps to compensate, said "Please call me Ferbo,
my pals do."

Ferbo in the office kitchen with Milos, the new guy

"Hey, Ferbo. Where did you bury him?"

"That wasn't necessary. I had a talk with Withers—
about his future, how one was still possible.
He'll be busy the next few days,
pulling at various shirt tails.
That pastrami looks good. You shouldn't eat it all yourself.
Look at your waistline.
Pass me a hunk of that bread and a butter knife.
Rummage around in that top drawer. Right. Thanks.
Hard to find a clean plate around here."

"Ferbs, they reckon it's gonna rain seven days straight,
starting tomorrow. I'm worried about my zucchinis.
Too much rain, you can get a slightly bitter taste…"

"Don't call me Ferbs! It's Ferbo—rhymes with "Turbo"—
get that straight or start looking for other work."

"Ok. Ok. Chill. Wait a sec. Here's a big jar of capsicums for you.
Pickled them myself. Give some to a neighbour.
They'll love you for it. I promise."

Autumn in New York II

End of Summer, but this is a foretaste of Autumn. Surely.

I drop in to the Park Lane Liquor Store.

Buy Strega. A bottle I'll have to carry across town.

Not that it's such a rough area—& it's bound

to have liquor—but *One anxiety at a time.* I'd train or

bus, if I knew Dee Dee's station—but it's the weather

for walking. I feel like it. And I'll arrive on time.

They'll have a while to talk before I get there.

Deed opens the door, & Marian's over by the window. "Where,"

says Dee Dee, "is your hat? Didn't bring it?" "I

feel like I'm impersonating myself, when I wear it—

especially with people who'll *remember* me in it.

What am I—a cartoon character?" I hand her the bottle.

"Alan, thank you," she says, & my nerves settle.

We *were* friends. And I *liked* her. I am forgiven—

for the long cooling off, the distance, tho truly

it was Deed & Marian were friends. I was a boyfriend.

And *came between them.* Or didn't. But witnessed things winding

down. Shame, embarrassment, awkwardness with every meeting.

Which became fewer. And she *moved.* When

35

she left the city for Newark—it was over.

Marian preferred to like Dee in memory. She's back now.

But an invitation marks something. I think she calls in

at the flower shop. Marian says they talk there for hours,

catching up—old times—news. So, 'back in town'.

Meanwhile

Meanwhile, whoever was murdering the great chefs of Europe
was murdering them still. Huston looked up to see
a body launch itself from the high-diving tower of the
circus, arms & legs outstretched like a frog or
glider-possum, away *from the tank—set for the purpose,*
below—& out towards the spectators. *If he did not*
think fast & act faster another chef would be dead & a mess
to clean up, the third this morning. He checked
his watch—11.30, wrote Grescu. This was easy.
'Leave 'em hanging' — he was positive he had heard that
before in relation to narration. No need to finish it either.
Just type it up & add it as 'support material' to
the application form, the grants were announced around Xmas,
Zoty had told him. In the bag. Markou was working on
his, too, at the kitchen table. "Dralex," Grescu addressed him,
"cup of tea?"

Some distraction needed

"I've been re-reading the manual HQ gave us—
certain phrases and codes related
to that beverage—coffee."

"Is it a lubricant, Galacto?"

"No, that's beer.
It's more of an accelerant."

"Are there side effects?
Yes—an immediate lift in mood,
possible flirting and joke-telling,
then eventual irritability."

"Sounds like beer to me."

"You've got a point there, Celesta.
Lordy, this planet. Nine Earth months here..."

SIXPACK FIVE

A Canberra conversation

"Scott, what do you know about Armenia?"

"Not a thing. Look it up in the medical dictionary."

"It's a not a disease, it's a country, silly."

"I don't like it when you call me silly, Peter."

"I did say it with affection."

"Not exasperation?"

"Well, I cannot tell a lie. I *am* a bit restless.
Can you and I go on some fact-finding mission?"

"What, to Armenia?"

"No. Somewhere warmer. Bali or Tahiti."

"Did you called me silly, again?"

"Whoops-a-daisy, maybe I did."

"Drink time?"

"Now you're talking!"

"I'll get the vodka out of the freezer…
Which reminds me, I should give Vlad a call.
Would *that* be silly?"

"No. Nope. No siree. Definitely not."

"In the hallway, is that new carpet? Are these Ikea glasses?
Keep pouring. Yeah, right to the brim. Thanks, Scott."

Call Me Mr Luck

Alan crosses with the lights, to the corner,
not much after five, he thinks, late sun enlivening the neighbourhood,
catching the trees—the undersides of the leaves flickering
in the intermittent, gusting wind.

                           A street-cleaner
disappears slowly round the far corner near
Marian's, comically elephantine, quietly noisy, if that's
possible. It has changed down a gear &, in the act of
disappearing, seems to be taking its noise with it. The street
looks transformed, the pale undersides of the leaves shimmer.

He passes the Goodwill store & sees it in the window.

"Hullo," says Marian when he enters. She is handling flowers,
long-stemmed & dripping, as she assembles & transfers them
from smaller to larger vases & buckets, sorting,
selecting out. She is wearing the yellow dress she wore
to the party at Dee Dee's—the dress a nice one
(she looks beautiful in it, he thinks, her skin like honey),
so today must have been special in some way.
It had been—a buyer for a group of restaurants
was there all morning, to make selections, place orders. "Dee Dee came,
you just missed her." "She okay?" "Yes. She thanked us

42

for helping on Friday. She thought it went well, that it mightn't
if we hadn't been there." "All we did was spin her records,
dance a bit, mix a drink or two." "Yes, but you know Dee Dee,"
said Marian. "She liked some of our friends." "I thought
she knew them all." "No, only Hayley & Luther.
Well, Esther she knows, has always known," she lifts a pail,
tall, narrow-necked, a firm base—"known her
since school." "You know the hat?" "Your old one?
Dee Dee was just talking about it." "It always made me look
slightly funny, didn't it? Innocent? A simpleton?"
"Nup. I love it." "The broad brim ..." "No, you looked
'blessed' in it, safe, charmed." "Right.
I gave it away. The Goodwill shop." "Why? You didn't."
"It really looked alright? It's still there, I could get it." "You should.
You look lucky in it."

On The Beach

"your troubles will be out of reach"

I come out of the water, dumped once—tho not badly—& having caught
a few waves—surfacing near some teenagers, all girls in their mid teens, a
younger brother amongst them. Brown, all of them, but no more tanned than
me. Less confused tho. Steadier on their feet. Make my way
up the beach—which is not too tightly packed. A Wednesday, lunchtime.

For a moment I think I've strayed while swimming—from where I was. There is
someone lying on a towel very close to mine. Asleep—sunglasses, book on her
chest. Why so close? The heavy silver bracelet I recognise, shake my hair
so the fine drops can wake her. "Frank," she says, opening her eyes, "How
very odd to meet you." "Strikes you that way, does it?" "Frank, yes, I'm sorry."

I pick up my towel, dry my hair, my chest & shoulders. "I feel like I'm
Matt Helm or someone—Tony Rome—& you're Jill St John, Eva Marie Saint,
& I'm James Coburn." "Frank, I don't know what you're talking about. These
people—are actors? you've gone back to the golden years of Hollywood?
Americana doesn't interest me." "I have reason to be annoyed with you," I tell her.

"I'm sorry for that, Frank. If you'd been *curious* enough

to travel to Melbourne, you'd have been barely inconvenienced: 'Lost Luggage',

for just one day—& I'd be a lot wealthier." "No decent beaches in Melbourne, Veronika.

And you advised me: walking in sand, you said, would cure it." "You are

walking much better," she says. We head off the beach, back to the cars, the streets.

I hand her my shirt, large, blue, suitable for Sydney suburbs. Her book:

English Biography of the seventeenth century by Vivian de Sola Pinto. "Why

are you reading this?" "I needed something. Picked it up in an 'Op Shop'

(I believe that is what they're called.)" "'Lives of the poets' sort of stuff, is it?"

"I'll learn something, Frank, even if it's just *what serious minded people*

were reading back in ... 1950." "I don't think any serious person took

Poetry seriously back then." "They seem to have, Detective."

She waves the book at him. "We quit, in the US, before the fifties."

"Is America a serious country, Frank?" "Vonnie, you shouldn't have come here.

I'm being watched, at least some of the time—& there are detectives out here

from Hawaii, Christ knows why—very keen to find you." "Okay." A pause.

"I need money, Frank, to get out of here. About twelve hundred." *"Me?"* I say—

surprised, but also touched. "Will your wife mind?" "I won't tell her for a while."

It seems I've already decided. "Look, move quick. Leave from Brisbane or somewhere—

not Sydney or Melbourne. The name they're pursuing, that they think you're using,

is Devereaux. *Don't* use that. They know Stein too." "Okay." "Don't fly into
the United States. Go to Mexico or somewhere. Drive across." "This
is a big favour, Frank." "Might not see you again," I suggest, firmly.
"Keep on with the legs," she told me, when we parted—on Arden Street
of all places. No-one shifty about, no Audi. "I will," I called, & turned—

up the hill at Coogee, to Michael & Di's, our Sydney friends. A shower.
Something *not* to tell.

Brenda remembers

Dad sang in the shower.
You could hear him all the way out in the kitchen.

"It Ain't Necessarily So"

"They Call the Wind Maria"

"The Surrey With the Fringe on Top"

He was in *hundreds* of productions.
From country theatres, community halls
to the Sydney Opera House.
He could turn on a penny, do the splits.
Looked carefree, performing
the most complicated dance routines.

It was me who found Dad, lying in the shower.
Shivering. A broken hip.

He was ten days in the hospital.
Yep, you guessed it, singing to the nurses.

"Love Letters in the Sand"

"What a Difference a Day Makes"

"Violets for Your Furs"

When he died there were so many cards and telegrams—
even one from Sir Robert Helpmann.

No, I don't need a tissue. Just give me a moment.
Deep breath. There. I'm ready, Iris.
The night is young. Let me grab my handbag.
You really think I look ok? Well, you look fab. Let's go.

Bridget and Tanya, the Top Dog Grooming Salon, Richmond II

I weakened. Slept with a man. The clincher?
Well, he's in a band called The Spatulas.
Yeah, not the greatest name.

His name's Fintan. No, no. Irish, not Asian.
Between his accent and the fact that he mumbles
I don't catch every word, but both of us
do a lot of talking with our hands.

The Spatulas are recording their debut album.
Fintan's noticed how I like reading so much
and wants me to come up with an album title,
says he wants "a real grabber." I'll run some by you—

Buckwheat Pancakes in the Sky
Too psychedelic? Not psychedelic enough?

Frog Socks
Intriguing, right? Sit with that one.

Bananas Comin' At Ya
Hints at a reggae vibe, which The Spatulas definitely have.

That's my short list.

Think about those three over the weekend and get back to me…

By the way I love your new hairstyle.

Brave of you to get it cut so short.

Where you'd get it done? Ah, at Tumi.

I had a falling out with that Zee, the owner.

I ran over her dachshund's front paws

while reversing the Kia SUV in Bridge Road.

Dog survived but not our friendship.

Boss, you could patch that. A present. Say some lingerie from

Passionfruit. Let's close the salon early, both go and take a look.

Marta Saulnier Considers

Her world is about to shrink.

Will she go see the Baldessari show? *Her commentary,* she knows,

all the words, will be for Chloe. Until now

distant & unimagined, it suddenly feels imminent.

A sudden narrowing, an end.

A relegation.

To one's self & to silence. What will she *like* when Chloe goes?

Anything? The cat? (There is none. She won't get one.)

So, a colder but roomier apartment.

Gardening (in pots?), painting, *watercolour?* Ha ha.

Television? Uh-uh. *Reading.* More than she

already did? Travel. Where, why? Alone? *Write?*

Research & write, she thought. Maybe that.

I could report to Chloe, & Nick.

Now. Stay in? Or be brave, go out. There is

nothing on her cell-phone. She looks again

down at the trees out her window—cars, parking, pulling out,

home to dinner. A calm light, no longer sun;

the wind has dropped.

SIXPACK SIX

Chloe waiting

"This is the beginning of a great adventure"

Chloe sits at one of the outside tables & looks
down the street. She is waiting—with no impatience—
for her boyfriend to arrive. Is he that? May be.
He will be punctual, about thirty minutes away. Justine
could arrive any time. Now? An hour hence?

And laden with bags probably, her eye captured by the area's
cheaper fashions. *Nick won't have so long to wait* ...
to meet this unmannered stranger. If he sees it that way. Marian's,
the florist's, is closing. Right on six. The yellow dress must be Marian.
Yellow, with irregularly spaced but regularly shaped

whorls of white—gardenias, shells, commas? The man 'with'
Marian has a number of hats, hands them to the woman
& takes the flowers from her. They are in a long metal can. Roses.
Chloe knows the woman to speak to. She closes,
usually, later—"or have I kept her back?" Tho Marian

had seemed happy, always, to have the girl there, buying

flowers for her mother, choosing slowly. Marian

had not been impatient: she liked the serious girl, she

liked her mother. Saulnier, was the name. Equally

serious. "Both of them," she thought—"'Gravitas'." Or was it a question

of solemnity—the Houynhym factor? She tipped well—

& un-ostentatious about it. Also the daughter. What was not to like?

The girl made a joke once that Marian remembered. The mother

always drily acerbic. At this moment Chloe's mother

is at home, feeling a little lonelier than she might,

her daughter interested in a Russian boy, Nick—Nikolai—impressed

with what she takes to be his Culture. Certainly he is serious.

But the culture Chloe credits him with—what can it be, the son

of a factory-worker father; a mother, who died when he was sixteen,

a cleaner? A student here, a little over twelve months. Nikolai—the inverse,

she thinks, of what she wants for her daughter. And to lose her—

something she thought she had worked towards all these years.

She will be old suddenly, alone. *Bitter*—she can feel it. How not?

Marian waves to her young customer, across the road,

to a curly-haired Adonis, & another girl, colourfully dressed—

high-piled red hair, large hoop earrings. Students of course. Different, each.

Acts of kindness

Sunday morning. Rani is standing on the top step of a ladder,
stringing Xmas lights along the roofline of the front verandah.

"Better early than curly," calls out Mr Ferber,
who's out walking his chihuahua.
He's crossed the road, to be certain of being within earshot—
"Rani. Give me a couple of hours.
I'll secure you some neon stars, maybe even a reindeer…
and oh yeah, a long power cord—
I've got pals in positions of *influence,*
though, in days gone past, some have been
'Indisposed Federally'
at very short notice…
Whoops, dog's pooed on your nature strip.
I'll pick that up later… See you again around 3pm.
You'll be impressed with what I bring back."

Rani watches Mr Ferber walk towards his silver Merc,
place Acapulco on the passenger seat.

Five years and Australian-English, its irregularities,
fresh volleys of slang and "street" phrases, continue to
baffle and intrigue Rani.
She thinks it'd be fun
to teach Mr Ferber, or Ferbo, as he prefers to be called,
some Shona and Malayalam—
perhaps a few words of greeting and politeness.
Ferbo has the look of a fast learner.

Release

A week, ten days, would go by and again Ferbo
would think about Shane.
There were rumours as to his whereabouts—
the Pilbara, Arnhem Land,
the Solomon Islands—there under a different name,
hair dyed black, living with a local woman, a kid on the way.

Revenge was tied up with saving face, tribal reputation.
Leaning on people. Erasure and disposal. The whole macho trip
no longer gave Ferbo that chest-beating surge.

His reality *had* changed over this last year.
He was now a home owner, a guy who
took afternoon naps, watered a garden,
had and enjoyed down time.
Ferbo's masseuse, Liza, had commented
that there was less tension in his shoulders.
He's told Liza that he taken up lawn bowls.

Shane had always been smart, probably remained so.
The seas, around the Solomon Islands,
were a continuous offering of blue.

Nice Pricing

A hit list, as his brother calls it, makes sorting much easier. Rahal
can look—not even focusing mentally—for certain shapes & materials
& especially certain brands & logos: Diet Coke cans are a handy one,
expensive 'cool' cosmetics, shave & after-shave containers. The rest,
clothing, appliances, foodstuffs, most toys & electrical equipment,
he can ignore. For some screw-on lids, certain kinds, you keep an
eye out. A bag full—still quite light—& you go home & cut
& assemble. It's like doing puzzles—fun—or a task as you get
tired of it. Rahal assembles mostly small, replica, model Daleks.
An occasional, one-off robot.
Not even hard. The tourists like them—the Brits, the Americans,
Europeans generally. They like them to be identifiably
made from refuse, & slightly ragged. Too good & they suggest
'Design' rather than ingenuity, their Mumbai or Kolkata origins.
You price them at a bit above what the other constructions go for—
the inventive bicycles, aeroplanes, steamships, rickshaws, monsters—
this gets their attention—brother Walid's idea.
He has a shower, eats with his mother, assembles his tools.
He cleans the various pieces now, his sister looking on.

You Again

"I remember wondering if he had paid his fare."

Bryan, one of the juniors, picks up his briefcase. "Hang on," he says.
"Just excuse me for a moment. I know that guy—I just
want a word with him," and he steps across the deck
to the man, standing, his back to her—as he watches … 'New York' pass by,
or the white-caps & choppy water created by their wake,
& the other vessels that cross their path.
She observes them talk, both, in that very male
way, facing out—to across the iron-grey water,
(out of the sides of their mouths? she wonders)—
silhouetted against the skyline & Tribeca.

Work, when she gets there, will be catch-up.
After three weeks away she feels closer to winding up
her partnership—a process that will take the best part of
a year, if she is not to inconvenience clients, & leave 'gracefully'.
A law firm, so she is hostage to conventions. *Be an
early exit,* she thinks, *at her age.* "Who were you talking to?" she asks,
& he says, standing beside her once again,
"His name's Ramon. I had to ask, myself.
I recognised him. We talked once

a while ago. I thought I knew that hat & coat.

Though they were different. But the same style." "'Downbeat'?"

"Yes. The first time I met him I thought he was a tramp."

"So there have been other times?" "No, but I've kept an

eye out." "Why?" "We got talking. Just because we were

standing there, side by side. He said something interesting. Advice,

I suppose, or an observation." "Be careful where you take

your counsel." "Ha ha," he laughed. "I really liked him."

"It's amazing how few times anybody ever says anything interesting, isn't it.
I hadn't noticed till I spoke to him that time."

"And on this occasion?"

"Not this time, no. But I'll be keeping an eye out."

"Yes, well. I suppose there's that."

Sitka, Alaska

Brief the summers here.

The sea, often a vast tantrum.

Monika in the back yard greenhouse, tending to her edible herbs.

This cabin, he'd built himself—

winching each rafter in place, tiling the roof.

Shane's former life—the close shaves—twice a gunshot wound,

his partner hauling him to the getaway car.

The wait in a railway hotel—

for that bent doctor, Knutsen, to climb the stairs.

The deep swim of morphine, the surgical digging

to locate and remove the bullet,

then the rough bandaging,

the hefty cash payment to the doc,

hoping for no infection.

Monika pops a cherry into her mouth, then one into Shane's.

The talk returns to whether they should buy a dog.

Monica opens up her laptop, shows Shane photos and breed details

of some of the mutts for sale.

They settle on an Alsatian—

excellent guard dogs.

SIXPACK SEVEN

Gill and Lenny talk while repairing a John Deere tractor

"Next month Frau Ginch
is going to be a hundred."

"She still smoke?"

"You bet, sits out on her porch
in minus ten degrees weather,
filling then lighting that clay pipe."

"She was a member of the gun club
until her eyesight went south.
That's the one time she's left the county—
to go to Omaha, get her cataracts done."

"Vern at the general store
figured she would have thought about
operating on herself,
using a hand mirror, a paring knife,
a sewing needle and cotton thread."

"Do you know anyone who's been *inside* her place?"

"Nope, not a soul."

"Reckon Claude from the funeral parlour
will be the first."

"We'll I'm not going to hold my breath waiting
for that to happen."

"Me, neither."

"Hand me that spanner."

"There. Done."

In For The Kill

'The French'll bet on anything' — old saying

"How many we got?" Clive asks of the pair. "Ten,"
says Dralex Markou. *"Eight, but I've still got some ideas,"*
says Grescu, *"—say ten for me too."*
"Getting late. What you've got will do. We run off
twenty copies of each—Not *long* are they? Not much
toner left. And I'll fill out the forms & we mail 'em
off." "Think we might win?" *"I might,"*
says Zoty. *"Not us tho? No chance?"*
"Sado, I'm the writer here. I'm paying *you."*
"It's been three days, Clive. I feel I'm becoming professional,"
says Grescu, & Markou laughs. "So what's the idea?"
he asks, stretching back in his seat. "We attribute
this stuff to the other writers—the usual short-list
characters—& send in numerous applications
under each name. You can only enter once.
They'll be disqualified. It'll be me & a few outsiders.
Level playing field." *"Outsiders?* So we should place bets?"

"Bets?" Zoty looks briefly surprised—& frowns. "No,
I don't think there'll be *that* much interest."
"Not like the Whitbread," says Sado Grescu. "Or the Man Booker,"
says Markou. *"Or the Prix Goncourt or the Prix Renaudot,"* says Grescu.
"Maybe we should take this idea there? The French'll
bet on anything."

Emma Stanley

You can see them as dears, or old dears, but it's not

the best way. Emma is doing a preliminary round

of the wards & an elderly woman, propped up against

pillows—a blue shawl, glasses, newspapers spread

before her—the *Australian*—says "I know you, dear." "No,"

says Emma, "it's my first day." "Then you're

the new matron?" says the woman, "Congratulations." "Oh.

Oh, you're *Mrs May,*" Emma recognises her patient.

"And you're Emma Balfour," says the woman.

"Emma Stanley," the nurse corrects her. "Quite.

You've *hardly changed.* You saved my life,

I gather. How long has it been?" "Since The Royal Melbourne?

Six years. A lot of us attended you. You pulled

through. You must be quite old. You look well.

Are you?" "Yes, dear. Ninety. I'm sure it says there.

I'm out of bed most days—not travelling very far.

And what have you been up to. Married?" "Yes."

"Children?" "A boy, he's four. Did you have children,

Mrs May?" "Call me Ellen, Emma. No, I never married."

"Oh? But I thought …" "The name, *Mrs May?* I preferred Mrs.

'Miss May' sounded like a pin-up." "Ha ha." "Or worse.

Bare-breasted. You know I was a gardener—

selling flowers, seeds, plants, advice." "My mother watched

your show." "Ha! And now you're here, in charge. Tell me. I wonder. You seemed to have your cap set for one of those young doctors. Did you marry him?" "Oh, no. Was it that obvious?"

"Not specially, dear. But I knew. I notice these things."

"I lucked out there. He's married to one of the other girls. I don't think they're very happy." "But you are."

"Yes, I am. Ellen, *I must go*. But I will see you again tomorrow." "Emma, who was the man ... in *The Good, The Bad, & The Ugly? Not* the handsome one." "Mrs May ..." "I know, I know. It doesn't matter. Eli Wallach!" "Good. I'll see you soon."

Darn that dream

Herman wipes the sweat from his forehead,

moves away from the jackhammer,

has a slurp of Diet-Coke.

Two sandwiches wrapped in wax paper.

There'll be no surprises there—

ham and pickle on rye.

Sometimes Greta puts a lemon cupcake

in his lunch pail, but not today.

She had looked tired at breakfast.

Up past midnight three nights in a row,

sterilizing glass jars, simmering honeyed syrup,

preserving the kumquats she'd gathered from the orchard.

From the back pocket of his overalls

Herman retrieves the creased brochures.

Would Greta appreciate a foreign adventure
or worry the whole time about pickpockets, gypsies,
open sewers and rabid street dogs?

Herman knows the answer.
They'll vacation in Florida.
Later tonight he'll telephone Greta's brother,
tell him to get the spare bedroom with ensuite ready,
be generous with the air freshener.

Examination

Amira pauses halfway down the street,

reaches into her dressing gown pocket,

recounts the coins.

Yes, the right amount

to buy two sausage rolls for dinner

from Finbar's, the corner shop.

Amira likes the tinkle of the bell on entering

and the bright packaging of the chocolate bars,

neatly arranged in the display cabinet.

There's Vivian, Finbar's daughter,

bent to a thick text book,

the wings of a notebook open,

thick-lensed glasses slipping a little

down her nose.

Amira sets down each coin deliberately,

from left to right on the counter,

while the drinks fridge hums.

"Mind the step," calls out Vivian

from the crease of her notebook,

to Amira's exiting back.

Amira's shuffle home

takes longer, being uphill.

She stops twice.

Once to smell a lavender bush

then to say a prayer for Vivian.

Cool

Emily & friend Carolyn walk, with a pack of kids, heading home,

seven boys up front, in two rows across the footpath, yelling, laughing,

pushing each other, making jokes—four girls behind, talking, half

an eye out for the boys' antics—*with* them, but staying clear.

The two drop back just a little, a trailing pair.

"I hope you don't go away *next* holidays. I was bored."

"What did you do?" "Nothing! I hung out with Sarah a bit.

& Maddy—but she went away as well. My brother just reads,

& rides his bike. He stopped talking about a year ago.

So, television." "Hmm. Still," said Emily, "no school." "I even studied,"

said Carolyn, "What about you? Adelaide any good?"

Emily tells her how small it is. "It seems to have everything though.

I mean, the usual stuff." "Anything cool?" "Cool enough. It's not Melbourne,"

she adds, "but I liked it. I was with my Aunt." "Oh. I'd have rather stayed home."

Emily says merely that *It was okay.* As they walk they are watching

the boys, who have quietened themselves. A few have peeled away.

The school day is ending. To be replaced by Home. She recalls Berys

& the walks they went on—once, sometimes twice a day—

her interest in her aunt's opinions, her aunt's interest in hers.

Her mind had come back home—after two weeks away—

quite a few years older, she felt. They had done nothing

in Adelaide, but talked & talked, had coffee & talked some more.
Berys bought her an expensive cardigan Emily's mum had been
impressed by. She felt much less certain about the world,
& much more certain she'd be alright in it.

SIXPACK EIGHT

Small Circus, Mountain Village, Nepal

You stand behind, taller than the group before you—an audience
of peasant farmers and workers, men & women, fine-boned, thin,
and a dozen or more small children—and, with them, gaze
at the long coffin-like box that has been mounted now two days
on the makeshift table. The table itself the village has supplied, in,

it would appear, a common form of advertisement: there has been,
all week, some stir around its presence. The coffin-like box, lidless, open side
to the audience, its back wall painted with a jungle scene
whose colours have dulled. It shows the dozen or so murmuring heads
a simple painted backdrop, as in vaudeville theatre. A conventional scene—of trees,

a meandering stream, a 'gypsy' caravan, striped yellow & blue, a dark red roof.
In each side wall of the box a hole has been cut. Finally an aged Chinese man, in
a 'coolie' hat, is standing behind the box and depressing a lever,
and a slow gamelan-style tune sounds. And stops. There has been no introduction.
The show has begun and the audience is quiet. He presses the lever again.

And once more the music sounds—and continues, faltering occasionally or dropping out,
but the theme is an unemphatic one & continuous, a little like the jungle background.
Thru the hole at one end of this tiny 'stage' a *very small monkey* (lemur? tamarin?) appears,
does a tumble, & another, & thus crosses the stage—
& out the hole at the other end—followed by a very small chicken—which does

much the same, circling upon itself one or two times—& a gerbil or guinea-pig.
They appear again, funnelled behind the box, back to their start, on the right, where they

        enter,

bashful, determined, uncertain, two further times. Then, controlled from behind,
a small, brightly painted wooden fox, legs spaced as if leaping, 'runs'—
from one end of the box to the other. It has 'chased' the animals.

The music stops. There is talk.

The Chinese man lifts his head & smiles patiently. Children make the odd,
querulous noise. You step forward & place a large coin, in the bowl, placed
for that purpose on the box. The coin provokes applause and sounds of approval.
The recipient nods a number of times, withdraws, returns,
to pack away equipment, place the animals on his cart,

which he starts & keeps in neutral
as he bumps down the hill.

The village has been served, has been visited.
They hear the motor engage a while later.

À la Rose Rouge, Saint-Germain des Prés, 10 October 1958

The club draws a varied crowd—
writers, painters, intellectuals, students from the Sorbonne,
nurses from the American Hospital,
and *every* night, Arcel and René, two of the district's street sweepers.

Several local players arrive. Push to the front. To be
floored again by Sonny's range of sound—
feathery, supple, propulsive,
able to honour the architecture of a standard...
but in the blink of a couple of bars,
unfold a new blueprint.

Sonny's glad that he's wearing the suit tonight
as there's Eddie, owner of Barclay Records, over by the bar,
writing out something in his notepad, maybe his phone number...

A ballad to start the second set.
The band begins "You Go To My Head"
which draws an immediate smile from Eddie.

Henri at the piano. His fingers stroll then slow—

hold the ladder steady for Sonny's climbing.

In walks Juliette. There are rumours about her,

how she threw a diamond engagement ring into the Seine.

Tonight Sonny *will* talk to her.

He'll need a couple of brandies first.

Closer each day

Yesterday in the soup kitchen
the serving volunteer
had slipped Albert a little extra—
two hard-boiled eggs.

He tapped the shell of one
against the steel pylon of the bridge.

What was stubble
when he started walking south out of Seattle
was now a beard.

Albert recounted
the coins and dollar bills
in his pocket. $29.85.

He remembered from last time
that San Diego was a good busking town.
He'd start with "Amazing Grace"
then follow with "Swing Low, Sweet Chariot"
finish with "You Are My Sunshine"
before any cops showed.

Albert knew an old mule trail
where he'd cross the border,
the next moonless night.

There was a cantina…
Albert hoped that Sanchez, the owner,
still had his accordion.
Thoughts of their reunion,
perhaps of forming a combo,
made Albert smile.

Jade

"Jada is my friend. She's in love with Al.
But Al don't love her, no no no—he's
in love with Sally, so, he's gonna break
her heart. When she drives up in that Volvo
& the horn begins to blow—I'm gonna
get out my chair, run down the stairs, &
open up that door.
'Cause, Jada is my friend. Don't want to see her
hurt again. Jada's got the biggest smile. Jada
is my lovin' chile." Etcetera.

She likes the simplicity of that line in the song,
& the happiness it can carry—'Cause, Jada
is my friend.
She empties the teapot carefully
over the pot plants. Returns & waters them all.
Her sister Ruth will call in.
The garden is looking nice. Overgrown,
but gorgeous. The canopy of green
filtering the light. She'll make scones.
In fact she has a present—earrings—
the small green stone among three silver leaves
looks beautiful.

Single Parent, Turramurra, 1962

Dot looks out the window & down onto the yard next door,
where Bob Arnold's white Holden is pulling up
& into their short straight drive.

●

I see Bob get out of the car. Bob Arnold. My husband
is another Bob. There are more. I'm Dot. A street
full of monosyllables—Bob, Joe, Jack, John, Sid,
Wal. Some of the women stretch to two. Lorna, Maree
(emphasis on the Maar). Bob gets out of the car &
looks up—a small voice has called, "Hey, Dad!"
& then, "Up here." Bob's daughter, Karen—aged ten?—
is high up the tree that stands just outside their house.
Bob puts everything down—his work bag, & what looks like fish-&-chips—
& calls out. "Are you alright? I want you to come down.
Careful." "I'm alright," the girl trills. "Slow, Aggie,"
he calls—his name for her. "Careful." The girl pauses,
& agonizingly reaches a leg down to a further branch.
It takes a seeming age, much coaching.
"Why did you let her up there?" Bob says to his son—
about two years older. "I didn't know," the boy says.

The girl down, Bob says, "You're never to do that again,
do you hear?" He picks up a rolled newspaper. The girl
evades his clutch at her, darts away—& off
down the side of the house, Bob giving chase. Bob,
unlike my Bob, a music teacher, large, diabetic,
short of breath, is fit & is gaining on the small blonde figure.
Around the back of the house Karen dives under the pipe
that leads from house to septic tank—a metre off the ground.
Bob must slow & crouch to get under. They circle the house
twice. The third time—as they round the corner,
come to the pipe obstacle again—her father begins to laugh
& Karen slows down & laughs with him. "Come here,"
he says, "you squirt." They hug. "You gave me
a fright," he says, as they go in, son carrying
work bag & dinner.

Curiosity

Ferbo no longer went bare-chested,

not even in the height of summer.

The scars, there on his chest and back,

had brought questions

from Kevin the postman,

Higgins, a neighbour,

from Bedders, that freckled dog-walking teenager.

Sometimes Ferbo had a beer

at the Esplanade Hotel,

but alone.

No one from a neighbouring table invited him

to hear about the ease or difficulty

of a recent "disposal".

That phone call, three weeks ago.

A woman named Valeria,

claiming that *he* was her biological father...

Ferbo worked the toothpick

between the best of his top teeth.

Yes, he *would* meet her. Somewhere neutral.
The Cellar Bar. Park the Merc some distance away.
He wouldn't wear the Rolex either.
Let her choose the wine.
His intuition and smarts—
Ferbo was going to need them.

He picked up his iPhone,
punched in the number.

SIXPACK NINE

At the Cellar Bar

Ferbo's wary.
But the wine helps.
He refills their glasses.

The wall mirror along the flank of the dining area
has already reflected their similar gestures—
the right hand sometimes
tugging at the left earlobe,
then looking off towards a framed poster, other diners,
before answering a question.

"You were weeks old, when I split.
There were forces at play,
approaching, ruinous.

My departure created attention but
that was what I wanted, a shift.

You have to believe—that
I thought of you and your mother
on hundreds of nights, in many places,
but contact would have been fatal.
You and I wouldn't be talking
here tonight if I'd weakened.

There's a lot to explain,
some of it shameful.
Please let me reveal myself
at a certain pace—
what I've been and haven't been…

Here, take a look at the menu.
Order a dessert. I'm diabetic,
another thing you didn't know about me.
Coffee, let's have that, a cognac too."

How I See Things

At first there Jimbo didn't sing. I'd wait
for it—but nothing. So I'd turn the radio on
see if that might get him started. All of this
meant I didn't regard him as my friend.
He was just a bird. Maybe he got to *like* me?
Maybe I changed my shirt. Anyway, he started.

Jim.

You don't know what they're thinking—
but it's best to assume they do. Who
wants to live with a moron?
Descended from dinosaurs, which we always thought
were dumb.
But parrots aren't, so maybe they weren't, either.
I'm thinking of a Brontosaurus, ruminating
like Heidegger, saying "This is the thing."

I ask Jim, What ist der Dichte und Sing?

Time to visit Waldo. My other friend.
I think Waldo … he doesn't so much
have friends, as acquaintances. He knows everyone.

And they all like him. He listens. He offers advice.

Me, I *like* a friend—but I only have one.
(Aside from Jim.)

Waldo.

Waldo

I rock up, he sees me coming
& puts down the planing tool he's working with
—planing, it goes without saying.
Unless he's just trying to protect himself.

"Still got that gun," I ask, "ha ha ha."
(I shouldn't shout that.)

"Sorry," I say—& as I get closer, "But have you?

You should sell it. I can sell it for you.
Not in Fitzroy. Further afield. *Who knows
what it's done."* "Yes. I know the theory," says Waldo.

"What brings you?" he says, "you look worried."
"The bird," I tell him. "What? Not working out?"
"No, no, it's begun to sing. I love his whole
little white person." "Good. Job done."

"Speaking of working out: I was at the gym the other night,"
I tell him. "You go to a gym?" He seems surprised.
"Yeah—& I'm lying there, doing stretches & such,
& this young fella comes in, just nearby,

& begins to punch the heavy bag. It's swinging around
quite near to me. Really laying into it. Setting it up
for good shots." "Frightening." "No, no. Just, it takes a while
to get used to.
I tell him, *Don't get him riled—*
don't get him mad. He looks at me for a few beats—
& he laughs. I thought, there, for a moment, I'd made a mistake.
But, no. Later, out in the car park
I'm looking for my bike—& I think, They've moved it.
I'm gonna get mugged." "For what you said?"
"Yeah. I'm thinking, *I wish I had that gun."*
"Necessary?" "No, just a thought.
Good joke tho, eh? 'Don't get him mad'?"
"I buried the gun," Waldo says.

                               "Figuratively,
or literally?" I ask him. "I think both," he says,
& laughs to himself at the thought. "*You're* in a good mood,"
he adds. "Yes," I say. "It's because of Jim."
"The bird? 'Jim' is it?" "Yes." And I tell him
my name for a new Greek disco star, Toxo Plasmosis,
& he laughs.

Valeria talks to Dr. Bernhardt

This man, my father,
his history comes self-censored
out of his thin-lipped mouth.

I look away
from his face,
fail to imagine
the number of identities
he's auditioned then discarded.

What can he give me?
Belated love?
I've searched for it elsewhere
for decades.

I know more about anger—
punched plaster walls,
slammed doors,
driving away
in another last legs car,
to some crappy motel,
adding to the cigarette burn marks
in the carpet.

Yes, I'll meet him again,

both of us

more adept at charm than truth.

But he's my father.

That counts for something, right?

I'm expecting you to tell me it does.

Clarissa talks with Elizabeth, 107 Powlett Street, East Melbourne

Sunlight arrives first to this side of the house, anoints the

odds and ends in that old cigar box. A faded stamp from

Formosa, a turquoise thimble, a pair of gold cufflinks which

Alex left with us. You remember him?

Well, after the fall of Singapore Alex made his way to India.

Ended up in Delhi. Heard Michaels, a chum from Cairo days

was there, importing Land Rovers. Hard to imagine Alex

behind a desk but he stuck it out for five years—then

quit abruptly, said he wanted to trek in the foothills,

visit the provinces. I think he said "every province."

After that, only rumours—

that he had a terminal illness,

was a volunteer in a Darjeeling orphanage,

may have been kidnapped by Kashmiri separatists...

His daughter, Dorothea lives here.

I suppose you'd call her a socialite.

Certainly not an adventurer like Alex.

I was in love with him for a while. You might have guessed.

Well, if you really want to know…

Wait a minute, I'll make a fresh pot.

'Leave them right there, Clint'

Bianca is finding her way into an essay—*thinking* only,
so far. About 'junctions' she remembers,
from old movies. In Westerns. There is *Getting off the horse*,
dismounting. This is a moment for initiating something:
the man will seek someone, announce himself, or ask
a question.

In submarine movies she always likes the ritual 'Periscope up',
'Periscope down' command; the scanning, the captain's
moment of decision or statement of a problem—a
stalemate or inaction. A crucial pause.

A woman will take off her earrings, or brush her hair.
Thoughtful. The woman considers herself, or considers
her problem—considers her state, often. Considers her state
more than considers her options.

This has been said before—so the point will be how Bianca puts it,
her wit with these categories … these instances, tropes, functions.

There are *windows*. Women look out a lot more windows than men,
in novels & films, in films especially: women confined,
women longing, women wondering—or just the contrast:
inner & outer worlds. She smiles briefly at the idea of

Clint Eastwood standing at a dressing table—removing an earring?
looking at his things, sighing? Marilyn—gets down from her
horse, strides purposefully, to the sheriff's office, to the small
important local paper. "I want to speak to the editor."

When a man hitches, she writes. *When a woman does …*
Then she thinks, *When a Girl Marries,* that old title.

Bianca remembers she has shoes to pick up. Still time
to get to the shoe repair. She 'mounts' her bike, laughs.

Notes

'Autumn in New York' is an earlier poem, featuring the same characters, in *The Elsewhere Variations*. Well, as well as being a song of Billie Holiday's.

'Mr Luck', a Jimmy Reed song.

'On the Beach'—a song first recorded by Eugene Boudin.

"The beginning of a great adventure"—Lou Reed, *New York Album*.

'You Again' connects with 'Aesthetics', a ferry-trip poem in *The Elsewhere Variations*.

Emma Stanley is a character who appears in 'Shifts', a poem in *Nearly Lunch*.

'Jade' begins with the lyrics, as remembered—of an early Pointer Sisters song, 'Jada'—from their first album, a decade before their fame began.

Bianca, in 'Leave them right there, Clint', writes an essay—for her Film Studies lecturer, Shannon Byrne, former television actor, American, not much given to theory, but, in the students' eyes (most of them), having the authority of experience. You didn't know that, did you? Byrne makes a number of appearances, too, in *Waldo's Game*.